Magical
Self-care Journal

Magical Self-care Journal

a guided journal to nourish and celebrate your body, mind, and spirit

Leah Vanderveldt

CICO BOOKS

LONDON NEW YORK

Published in 2021 by CICO Books
An imprint of Ryland Peters & Small Ltd
20–21 Jockey's Fields   341 E 116th St
London WC1R 4BW   New York, NY 10029

www.rylandpeters.com

10 9 8 7 6 5 4 3 2 1

Adapted from *Magical Self-care for Everyday Life*, first
published by CICO Books in 2020

Text © Leah Vanderveldt 2021
Design and photography © CICO Books 2021
Picture credits: Photography by Belle Daughtry, except
pages 9, 68 top left & 79: Gary Crabbe/Enlightened
Images/Alamy Stock, and pages 88 top left & 91:
Nuclear_xonix/Adobe Stock

A CIP catalog record for this book is available from the
Library of Congress and the British Library.

Flexiback ISBN: 978 1 80065 061 9
Paperback ISBN: 978 1 80065 080 0

Printed in China

Commissioning editor: Kristine Pidkameny
Editor: Martha Gavin
Senior designer: Emily Breen
Art director: Sally Powell
Head of production: Patricia Harrington
Publishing manager: Penny Craig
Publisher: Cindy Richards

Safety note: Please note that while the use of essential
oils, herbs, incense, and particular practices refer to
healing benefits, they are not intended to replace
diagnosis of illness or ailments, or healing or medicine.
Always consult your doctor or other health professional
in the case of illness, pregnancy, and personal sensitivities
and conditions. Neither the author nor the publisher
can be held responsible for any claim arising out of the
general information and practices provided in the book.

Contents

Introduction

Creating a self-care practice that will genuinely fill your cup is a matter of knowing yourself and feeling into the present moment. A magical self-care practice is one that includes your spiritual wellbeing as well as your physical, emotional, and mental wellbeing and brings an element of fun.

To believe in magic is to choose to see the world around you in a certain light—one that helps, encourages, and supports you. Magic invites us to entertain a change in perception and thought. Changing the way we talk to ourselves, the way we approach our needs, or how we interpret events can create shifts in our lives that sizzle with possibility—for our internal life and our communities.

Magical living gives us an opportunity to claim our power, make the changes we seek, and create a life that lights us up. And the best part is, you already have everything you need within you at this very moment.

Self-care is simply the practice of treating yourself well, but the phrase is a little fraught these days. There's a commodification of self-care that brings with it privilege and exclusivity, but that's not the kind of care we're exploring in this journal.

Some people think they're too busy, tired, or low on funds to take part in it, but self-care belongs to everyone—and it's especially important if you feel stretched thin. Self-care is typically portrayed as the surface-level stuff that you can spend money on. There's nothing wrong with serums, massages, green smoothies, or whatever else you buy when you want a pick-me-up, but a lot of these things don't help us feel the way we want to feel at our core.

Real self-care is about what we do little by little every day to nourish our bodies, minds, and spirits so we can show up as the best version of ourselves (and be okay when we're not feeling our best). It is made up of the practices, activities, and habits aimed at making us feel good at our core and bringing us back into balance. Often the foundational self-care—hydration, eating well, getting enough sleep, and connecting with others—can be the springboard for more expansive, mystical forms of self-care. Without these basics in place, none of the other magical practices in this book will be as potent.

Magical self-care is the practice of using rituals and tools that might be considered mystical, witchy, or esoteric to identify and address your needs. It requires being inquisitive, diving deep, and trusting yourself and your instincts. This process of self-care combines the grounded and the spiritual for personal evolution and healing.

It's about creating a better relationship with yourself through curiosity, awareness, and intention. Magical self-care asks you to develop a deep trust in yourself to help you discover what's best for you on a holistic (physical + mental + emotional + spiritual) level. It's about unlocking your own personal brand of intuition and magic by getting in touch with yourself, your worth, and your power.

How to use this journal

Your experience with this journal should ideally feel playful, exploratory, and fun. Approach the exercises with an open mind and be willing to get weird. This is just for you.

The purpose of this journal is to really put the power back in your hands, heart, and intuition. To get your mind and instincts working in new ways so that you can find the self-care that truly works for you. Only you hold the right answers for you. All of the tools and modalities shared in these pages are meant to support you in exploring and finding those answers in a new way.

There's a certain magic that happens when you put actual pen to paper. Our brains are able to synthesize information in a direct way and we open up a channel to our hearts by using our hands. (The hands are considered an extension of the heart in many healing practices.) When we let ourselves write freely, things can emerge that we never could have articulated otherwise. So let your writing flow without editing or censoring yourself.

RITUALIZE IT. Setting up a sacred space to do your journaling can create a physical and energetic container to do your work in. Before you dive into any of the chapters, practices, or exercises, consider taking a few minutes to set up your space. Find a cozy place to sit, gather water, tea, or snacks, and any crystals or mystical tools you love. Play calming music. Light a candle and open up your circle for communicating with your intuition. You can dance or move your body beforehand. Or meditate. Or do some breathwork. Use the tools that you discover in this journal to help you develop new rituals for yourself that feel energizing and resonant. If something doesn't feel like your thing, don't do it. If something piques your interest, give it a try.

USE YOUR MYSTICAL TOOLS. Weave in the witchy throughout your journaling experience. If you're into tarot like I am and find yourself stumped on a question, pull a card for it and use that as a jumping-off point for your answer. Many of these questions can be turned into tarot spreads or queries for you to explore and inquire from a different perspective. Similarly, look to the moon cycle to reflect on certain themes or try leaning into breathwork or an embodiment practice if answers aren't coming through. Sometimes we need to shift our energy to access our deeper truths.

PLAY. Believing in the magical encourages a sense of wonder and playfulness that we can easily lose sight of as adults. Exploring these magical ways of living is meant to infuse joy and excitement into the everyday, so don't be afraid to embrace that. Find ways to play with these practices and modalities in ways that light you up. That will be the path to finding what feels the most fulfilling and restorative for you.

CHAPTER 1

Embracing the Feminine

Regardless of gender, we all possess the masculine and feminine within us. Embracing the feminine is another way of saying embrace your internal world of feeling, listening, and receiving. It's the realm of intuition, nurturing, creation, cycles, and interconnectedness.

The terms masculine and feminine exist beyond gender, but if these terms are too binary for you, I invite you to think of them as external and internal.

How does the feminine (or internal) show up in your life?

How does the masculine (or external) show up in your life?

What aspect of your feminine side feels neglected? What aspect of your masculine side feels overactive?

Think about the last time you said yes to something that you really wanted to say no to. How did it feel and what was the outcome?

What does your energy look like throughout a typical day? Describe it, starting with how you feel when you get up through to when you go to sleep. This is your daily cycle.

AM

PM

To help you get to recognize your daily energy pattern, reflect on:

What did you learn about your energy on this particular day?

When did you feel your energy was at its highest?

When did you feel calmest?

When did you feel most strained, tired, frustrated, or overwhelmed?
These are times when you're being called into your feminine.
What would that look like for you?

**Just like you kept track of your daily energy cycles, it's important
to recognize your weekly and monthly rhythms to get a fuller picture
and to expand your self-care.**

Using the same prompts as on page 17, observe what your energy looks like
throughout the week. This is your weekly cycle.

Monday

Tuesday

Wednesday

Thursday

Friday

Saturday

Sunday

WEEKLY REFLECTION:

What does your energy look like throughout the month? Track it for four weeks. This is your monthly cycle (if you're a person who menstruates, you can also track your menstrual cycle here, as it may affect your energy).

Week 1

Week 2

Week 3

Week 4

MONTHLY REFLECTION:

Review the feelings of strain, exhaustion, frustration, or being overwhelmed that you wrote about on page 17. The next time they come up, what could you do to come back to your inner wisdom? What would help you rest and reflect?

What is one small change you can make to your routine that would engage your feminine side?

Embodiment is the practice of feeling your body and everything that's stored inside there. It can look different for everyone but usually involves movement and breathing.

Make a list of things you can do to get present with your body.
For example, try dancing, hip circles or swaying, intuitive stretching, deep belly breaths or breathwork, making sounds—sighs, shouts, laughs—anything that wants to come out of you.

Your body is your ally.

Embracing the Feminine in Your Everyday Life

It doesn't have to be all Goddess circles and meditation. There are plenty of grounded ways to get more in step with your feminine side. To get in touch with your inner wisdom, you must honor your body. Nurture yourself by asking your body what it needs and actually listen to what it's communicating to you. It's often the simplest things that we need the most. When the body feels properly fed, watered, and rested, it's easier for us to connect to our intuition.

Embracing the feminine can look like:

- Getting enough rest
- Drinking plenty of water
- Nourishing your body with foods that feel good to you
- Feeling your emotions fully
- Honoring the cycles of your body
- Having a daily pleasure practice
- Focusing on the five senses
- Asking your intuition questions
- Meditating to calm the overactive mind
- Breathing intentionally
- Movement such as hip circles, dance, and stretching
- Waiting to respond to circumstances rather than pushing them along
- Graciously receiving compliments, praise, and resources

Your body is always trying to help and communicate to you; it's time to start listening more closely. Ask your body: How do you feel today?

_____

_____

_____

_____

_____

_____

_____

_____

_____

_____

_____

_____

How can you honor your body today?

_____

_____

_____

_____

_____

_____

_____

_____

_____

_____

_____

Engaging with your senses is a great gateway into receiving.

What can you see right now? What can you hear? Smell? Taste? Feel?

What's an activity you can do today to activate your five senses in an enjoyable way? For example, eat a great meal. Plan not only the food, but also the ambiance, the music or sounds you'll hear, the place you'll sit.

Your senses invite you back
into the present moment.

Intuition expresses itself differently in each of us and in various ways depending on the situation. Some of us are gut feelers, others feel it in their chest. You can get chills, or hear simple words or phrases.

How do you hear or feel your intuition?

_____

_____

_____

_____

_____

_____

_____

Think back to a time when you clearly heard your intuition.
What was that experience like? Did you follow the information
you received from it? What was the outcome?

_____

_____

_____

_____

_____

_____

_____

_____

_____

We learn to listen to and strengthen our intuition when we engage with it regularly.

Write a list of questions you can ask your intuition daily. (For example, coffee or tea? What would feel best to wear today? What tasks would feel best to do first?) Next to each question write the first answer your receive for each. These are your intuitive answers.

Question	Answer

List all the things that bring you pleasure and joy.

How could you add more pleasure and enjoyment into your routine?
What would that look like realistically?

Use your intuition to plan out a pleasure ritual for each day of the week.

Monday

Tuesday

Wednesday

Thursday

Friday

Saturday

Sunday

In addition to sleep, what does rest look like to you? How can you make time for more rest—even if it's just an extra 5 minutes? (Hint: Put down your phone and laptop.)

_____

_____

_____

_____

_____

_____

_____

_____

_____

_____

_____

_____

_____

_____

_____

_____

_____

Only you know the right balance for you.

Envision how your life might shift when you invite your more internal/feminine qualities to guide you. Consider the ebb and flow of the two energies working together—how will it feel? What will it look like?

CHAPTER 2

Mirroring Nature & the Seasons

Paying attention to the rhythms of the seasons and nature is essential for our health, happiness, and sense of connection. If you feel at a loss as to what you need or how to care for yourself, simply look to nature as your guide.

What's your favorite place in nature? Describe it in detail.

How does this place make you feel?

What qualities of yourself are mirrored in this place in nature?

How can you put more emphasis on these qualities in your day-to-day?

Each season holds its own magic. Working with these energetic and physical shifts throughout the year is an easy way to start harnessing this magic.

What does spring feel like to you? What are the tastes, smells, sights, and sounds? What do you feel pulled to do during this time?

What does summer feel like to you? What are the tastes, smells, sights, and sounds? What do you feel pulled to do during this time?

What does fall feel like to you? What are the tastes, smells, sights, and sounds? What do you feel pulled to do during this time?

What does winter feel like to you? What are the tastes, smells, sights, and sounds? What do you feel pulled to do during this time?

How can you connect to nature regularly? Make a list of all the big and small ways you can ground yourself in the nature you have access to.

When in doubt, look to nature.

Whether it's for an afternoon, a weekend, or more, pick a time to turn off your social media, email, and news apps, or shut off your phone entirely. Technology is wonderful, but our devices are keeping us from fully engaging with the world around us.

Observe what you feel and notice without the technology, and write about it here.

Explore the Elements

Each of the four elements can be found in nature and are reflected back to us in many forms. The elemental system pops up as a framework in everything from tarot to astrology to house magic. The elements are a great introduction to magic. If you're creating an altar (see page 66) or working a spell, consider including something that represents each element.

WATER

Meaning: Our feelings, intuition, emotions, and inner world.

Immerse yourself: Get to or near the ocean, a lake, pond, or river. Dive in a pool, cry, take an extra salty bath, or create a sacred shower ritual.

Zodiac signs: Cancer, Scorpio, Pisces

EARTH

Meaning: Our purpose, self-worth, work, abundance, and receptivity.

Immerse yourself: Explore the woods, squish in mud, get lost in a park, look up at big trees and feel the grass beneath your feet, picnic, garden, or roam.

Zodiac signs: Taurus, Virgo, Capricorn

AIR

Meaning: Our thoughts and the ways we communicate.

Immerse yourself: Simply breathe it in and notice the shifts in it during different times of year, get up in the mountains or in an open field, coast your bike down a hill, or let yourself explore a new place without agenda.

Zodiac signs: Gemini, Libra, Aquarius

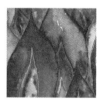

FIRE

Meaning: Our creativity, vitality, motivation and drive, movement, and sexuality.

Immerse yourself: Seek out the desert, tropical heat, simply soak in the sunshine, or hop into a sauna. Do movement that ups your energy and makes you sweat.

Zodiac signs: Aries, Leo, Sagittarius.

Which elements and environments are you the most drawn to?

Which element do you feel like you have the most of? The least? What would it look like to find a balance between all the elements?

The Wheel of the Year marks the shifts of nature and the corresponding energetic changes. In the following section, I invite you to create your own rituals and celebrations based on each holiday's theme. Include seasonally appropriate foods and plants, if that interests you.

VERNAL OR SPRING EQUINOX (MARCH 20)
Theme: New beginnings.
How would you like to honor this day?

_____

_____

_____

_____

_____

_____

_____

_____

What's ready to spring forth in your life?

_____

_____

_____

_____

_____

_____

_____

_____

_____

Embody Mother Nature.

MAY DAY/BELTANE (MAY 1)
Theme: Bursting into bloom.

How would you like to honor this day?

How can you celebrate and honor your body, mind, and spirit connection
in an enjoyable way?

SUMMER SOLSTICE/LITHA (JUNE 21)
Theme: Celebrating life and light.

How would you like to honor this day?

How can you sink into presence more in this very moment?

LAMMAS (AUGUST 1)
Theme: Savoring the fullness.

How would you like to honor this day?

What are you most proud of in your life right now?

AUTUMNAL EQUINOX/MABON (SEPTEMBER 21)
Theme: Shedding what's no longer serving you.

How would you like to honor this day?

How are you transforming? What needs to be shed to aid your transformation?

HALLOWEEN/SAMHAIN (OCTOBER 31–NOVEMBER 1)
Theme: Honoring life and death/the life cycle.

How would you like to honor this day?

What's coming to an end in your life right now? How can you honor that?

WINTER SOLSTICE/YULE (DECEMBER 21)
Theme: Going inward.

How would you like to honor this day?

_____

_____

_____

_____

_____

_____

_____

_____

_____

_____

_____

_____

_____

What will make this cocoon time of the winter nourishing and nurturing for what you really want to create in your life?

_____

_____

_____

_____

_____

_____

_____

_____

_____

_____

_____

_____

IMBOLC (FEBRUARY 1)

Theme: Nurturing the seedlings.

How would you like to honor this day?

How can you tend to your hopes and dreams while doing the same for
your body, mind, and spirit?

What is the theme of this current season for me? How does that align or not align with the energy of the natural season?

_____

_____

_____

_____

_____

_____

_____

_____

_____

_____

_____

_____

_____

_____

_____

_____

_____

Everything has a season.

CHAPTER 3

Creating a Magical Home

A magical home is a space that helps you come back to yourself and makes you feel good. The goal is to create a calming, grounding, and safe energy that supports you and helps you be your most authentic self when you step through the door.

What energies (positive, negative, and neutral) are currently
at play in your home?

_____

_____

_____

_____

_____

_____

_____

_____

_____

_____

What would it feel good to let go of and why?

_____

_____

_____

_____

_____

_____

_____

_____

_____

_____

_____

_____

In an ideal world, what would walking into your home after a long day look like to you? What would it feel like?

Use this space to set a few intentions for your home.

What areas could do with some decluttering?

After decluttering, you can energetically cleanse your space using smoke (burning dried herbs), essential oil sprays, sound, salt, and fresh air. Which of these appeal to you? Could you make your own essential oil spray, a cleansing bundle with fresh herbs, or playlists for shifting the energy? Write your ideas here.

To create a magical space, we must first cleanse and clear (through cleaning, decluttering, and energetic cleansing) and then we can enhance the environment with color, lighting, crystals, arrangement, and more.

Make a plan, room by room, of what needs to be cleansed and what you'd like to add to enhance each space.

Enhance and Create a More Aligned Energetic Space

Scent

Scent can change the feeling of a room. Try essential oils like sweet orange, neroli, and grapefruit for uplifting, lavender and sandalwood for chilling out, and peppermint and rosemary for improving your focus and easing tension and heavy energy.

Crystals

While crystals won't solve your problems for you, they do bring certain vibrations and can reinforce your intentions by holding space for them and serving as a visual reminder of what you're calling in or changing. The best way to pick the right crystals out for you is simply recognizing which ones you're attracted to. You'll be drawn to the right crystals for your home and life.

HERE IS A LIST OF CRYSTALS AND THEIR PROPERTIES TO GET YOU STARTED

Black tourmaline: clears negativity, removes bad thought patterns, reduces impact of electromagnetic radiation from cell phones and computers, reduces stress

Citrine: optimism, creativity, confidence, sunshine

Selenite: cleanses, clears, protects, light bringing, guidance

Smoky quartz: letting go, harmonizing, detoxifying, focus

Amethyst: spiritual connection, intuition, protection, anxiety reducer

Carnelian: ignites passion, but don't keep near your bed when you want to sleep as it can boost your energy

Celestite: healing sleep and gentle dreams, deeply calming, antidepressant, universal wisdom

Moonstone: divine feminine energy, soothing, balancing

Rose quartz: warm and fuzzy loving energy, coziness, calming

Green aventurine: stress and anxiety, brings luck, heart opening, connects you to healing Earth energy

Clear quartz: clarity, focus, healing, enlightened thinking

Labradorite: curiosity, universal connection, magic, clairvoyance, psychic abilities

Lapis lazuli: awareness, wisdom, soul purpose, guidance

Sodalite: aligning with your purpose, communication, intuition, organization

Music

Music can change the energy of a space. Create a few playlists for different moods and times (cooking music, meditation, date night) to conjure up a specific ambiance quickly.

Lighting

Natural lighting during the day and low lighting once the sun has set helps your body clock find its natural rhythm. You can use incandescent bulbs, small table lamps, twinkle lights, and candlelight in combination for your ideal glow.

Color

Color can have a huge impact on your mood, which makes sense because each color holds its own magic. Choose a couple of colors to form the base palette of your home and incorporate a power/accent color to weave throughout. You can do this room by room or for the home overall. Color meanings can be very individual to each person, so take these following associations only as a jumping-off point.

COLOR MEANINGS

Red: vibrance, security, passion

Orange: creativity, motivation, energy

Yellow: warmth, happiness, intelligence

Green: grounded, earthy, serene, abundance

Blue: calm, communication, wisdom, peace

Indigo: spirituality, rebelliousness, playful

Purple: dreams, psychic connection, power

Pink: love, tenderness, joy, kindness

White: clean slate, peace, intuition

Gold: luxury, warmth, abundance

Black: grounded energy, protection, stress banishing

Grey: soothing, softness, balancing

Silver: lunar energy, intuition, emotional balance

Coral: playfulness, cheer, positive energy

Turquoise: loving, open-heartedness, optimism

What colors are in your home? What do they mean to you?

Is there a color that you love that would add something special to your space?
What would that color enhance for you and how could you incorporate
it into your home?

What kinds of scents are you attracted to (floral, earthy, woody, spicy, musks, etc.). Which ones are a part of your lifestyle now and in what ways?

How do those scents feel in your body?

What kinds of things do you have hanging on your walls?

Is there a kind of artwork that you wished you had or something that would better express your passions or interests?

What is your relationship to your kitchen? How does it serve you?

How do you approach cooking and food? Is there a way to make your experience more mindful and magical?

The intention you put into your food is just as important as the ingredients.

Think of your favorite meal or dessert. Describe it in detail. How does it make you feel?

How do you want to feel on a daily basis? Try infusing these intentions into your meals before you serve and eat them. Do you notice a difference?

Altars are spaces that remind us of our intentions. They can be where we do magic, meditate, or just take a moment to re-center. The most important part is how you choose to decorate them.

If you don't already have one, where could you set up your altar space and why did you choose this location? (You can have multiple ones throughout the house!)

_____

_____

_____

_____

_____

_____

_____

_____

What kinds of objects would help remind you of your intentions for your home? Think outside the box here!

_____

_____

_____

_____

_____

_____

_____

_____

Grounding is the practice of coming back to the present moment and it's especially helpful when we spend a lot of time in our minds or "up in the air."

Choose a room in your home where you do something that helps you come back to your center and into the present (for example, in the bathroom, a hot shower helps you melt away stress from the day). Then list one thing you can tweak to make it more grounding (for example, make a lavender salt scrub to physically and energetically exfoliate the day away and calm down).

Your space supports your self-care.

CHAPTER 4

Lunar Living

Lunar living is moving through the world in alignment with the moon cycles. It's being aware of what phase the moon is in and the effect it has on you personally—and planning accordingly.

What, if anything, do you know or believe about the moon?

How do you feel when you catch a glimpse of a big full moon or a gorgeous sliver of a crescent moon hanging low in the sky?

The moon represents shifts and cycles, what we need to thrive, intuition, and our emotional nature. Think of the moon governing the tides and the similar impact it can have on our inner world.

How do you navigate life's ebb and flow? Are you attuned to your moods and emotions or do you resist them?

What's your relationship to your intuition? Do you make space to listen to it? How could you check in more?

Getting to Know the Moon's Phases

The Moon spends about 3½ days in each of these phases.

NEW MOON

The start of a new cycle. This is the time when the moon isn't visible in the sky—a blank slate. It's a time of beginnings, fresh starts, and new energy.

Use it for: Reflecting, restoring, and setting intentions for the cycle/month ahead. The intention that you choose will be your main focus throughout the rest of the phases, but if nothing comes to you on the new moon, just wait a couple of days. You can adjust and edit that intention as needed—in fact, the moon encourages that.

Simple action: Turn inward.

WAXING CRESCENT

The moon has grown into a pretty crescent at this time and the energy for supporting your intention is building.

Use it for: Feeling into your intention. Relax and see how your intention feels in your life right now. Where is it aligned? Not aligned?

Simple action: Feel into it.

FIRST QUARTER MOON

We're halfway to the Full Moon now and gaining momentum with our intention.

Use it for: Following that momentum you're feeling. During this time you may want to reach out and connect with someone who might need your help or just a kind word.

Simple action: Take action on your intention and show up for others.

WAXING GIBBOUS

The moon is almost full in the sky—energy is heightened and there is a palpable excitement.

Use it for: Looking back on the time that's passed since the New Moon and assessing what's working and what isn't.

Simple action: Take note of how the actions you've taken have landed. Adjust as needed.

FULL MOON

The moon is at its most brilliant and attention-grabbing at this time. You might feel the same—wanting to get out there and socialize, connect, or share what's in your heart and on your mind. You could also feel more emotional or intense than usual. This is an expansive time—whatever it makes you feel, fully show up for it.

Use it for: Celebrating the cycle so far, everything that you've worked on, and everything you're releasing. A celebration can be something small like an intentional meal or a gathering with friends.

Simple action: Share and release.

WANING GIBBOUS

The moon is slowly beginning to decrease from its full size. You might feel emotional after the high of the Full Moon or the pull to recharge.

Use it for: Feeling into the changes you've made so far and anything you've released. How does it feel to let go a little? It's okay to grieve whatever is changing and transforming.

Simple action: Recharge.

LAST QUARTER MOON

We're at that half-moon point again—paring back toward the New Moon and continuing to shed volume and light.

Use it for: Examining your boundaries. Are you shedding the things you don't need? What does that look like for you? Do you need to put a new system in place to help you?

Simple action: Say no.

WANING MOON OR BALSAMIC MOON

The moon is diminishing in the sky, preparing for a new cycle, but still finishing the current one. This period of time includes the Dark Moon in the day or so before the New Moon, which can be a particularly low-energy, introspective time.

Use it for: Feeling your feelings. You can feel physically drained around this time. Be kind and gentle with yourself.

Simple action: Reflect with release.

To start working with the moon as your guide, all you have to do is start checking what phase the moon is in, then noticing how you feel. Choose a time you can follow the moon through its full cycle. In the following pages, keep track of your thoughts, ideas, feelings, and intended actions during each phase.

New Moon thoughts, ideas, feelings, actions:

_____

_____

_____

_____

New Moon intention:

_____

_____

_____

_____

_____

There's always an ebb and flow.

Waxing Crescent thoughts, ideas, feelings, actions:

_____

_____

_____

_____

_____

Waxing Crescent intention:

_____

_____

_____

_____

_____

First Quarter Moon thoughts, ideas, feelings, actions:

_____

_____

_____

_____

_____

First Quarter Moon intention:

_____

_____

_____

_____

_____

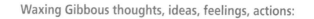

Waxing Gibbous thoughts, ideas, feelings, actions:

Waxing Gibbous intention:

Full Moon thoughts, ideas, feelings, actions:

Full Moon intention:

Waning Gibbous thoughts, ideas, feelings, actions:

Waning Gibbous intention:

Last Quarter Moon thoughts, ideas, feelings, actions:

Last Quarter Moon intention:

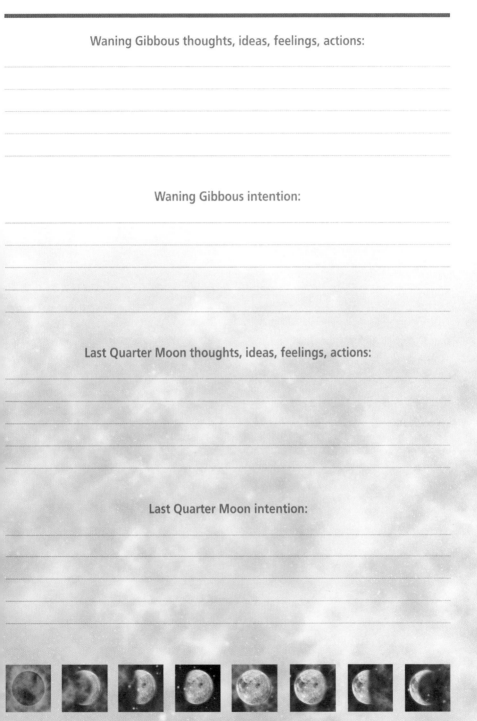

The Waning or Balsamic Moon is the day or two before the New Moon when we don't see the moon in the sky. This can be a low-energy, withdrawn time when we're being asked to tend to our inner world.

Waning/Balsamic Moon thoughts, ideas, feelings, actions:

_____

_____

_____

_____

Waning/Balsamic Moon intention:

_____

_____

_____

_____

List some comforting self-care ideas for the Waning/Balsamic Moon.

_____

_____

_____

_____

_____

_____

_____

_____

Your senses invite you back
into the present moment.

Rituals at the New Moon and Full Moon can be potent portals to self-inquiry and transformation. Based on how you personally feel in both of these phases, think about what you'd like your rituals to help you do (your ritual objective) and what activities or practices will help you achieve that. Consider what will help you be present and tuned in and what themes you would like to explore.

The objective of my New Moon Ritual is:

My New Moon Ritual could include (list any special practices or activities that you think would help with your objective):

Questions to ask at the New Moon:

What was the lesson of this past moon cycle?

What feels aligned to focus my energy on at this time?

What's my intention for this cycle and how does it support me physically, mentally, emotionally, and energetically?

What's feeling really good in my life? Not so good?

The objective of my Full Moon Ritual is:

My Full Moon Ritual could include (list any special practices or activities that you think would help with your objective):

Questions to ask at the Full Moon:

Where am I feeling out of balance in my life?

What's my intention for this cycle and what is holding me back from fully stepping into my intention?

What part of me wants to be seen and heard?

How can I celebrate myself this week?

Write about a pivotal time in your life.

What about the events of this time felt scary? What felt freeing?

What was the outcome?

How did that lead you to where you are today?

Change takes time.

What are you actively trying to change in your life?

What about the change is difficult to do? Where do you feel resistance and fear?

How could the ebb and flow of the lunar cycle support you in making these changes? List the best times to take action and the best times to rest, check in, and receive, and what that would look like for this specific intention/change.

CHAPTER 5

Self-awareness with Astrology

You're made up of so much more than your Sun sign (the zodiac sign you usually read your horoscope for). Accessing your birth chart can help show you the connections and complexities that are completely unique to you. For this section, look up your birth chart (also known as a natal chart) on astro.com. You'll need your birth time and place, in addition to the date. For most of this chapter, we'll be focusing on your Sun sign, Moon sign, and Rising or Ascendant sign (AC).

Your Sun sign is the one you're likely already familiar with. The Sun sign is who you are at your core and represents what wants to be expressed in your lifetime.

Write everything you think you know or have been told about your Sun sign.

What feels like you? What doesn't?

Keeping your Sun sign in mind, what would feel like the most "you" thing you could do in the present moment?

The sun is what everything
is centered around—
it's your core.

Your Moon sign is a reflection of the things you need to feel secure and cared for and your emotional nature. If you're unfamiliar with the qualities of this sign, you can look them up on page 98.

What feels like you? What doesn't?

Were there any surprises or things that you're already aware of about yourself?

If you put your Moon sign in the context of what you need to feel cared for, what does that look like to you?

Keeping your Moon sign in mind, how could you deeply nourish yourself today?

Your Rising sign is your outer shell, how you move in the world, and what you're here to cultivate. If you're unfamiliar with the qualities of this sign, you can look them up on page 98.

What feels like you? What doesn't?

Were there any surprises or things that you're already aware of about yourself?

How do you move in the world like your Rising sign? What outward qualities or sense of purpose can you see mirrored in your Rising sign?

Keeping your Rising sign in mind, what do you need to balance or cultivate more of to help you on your way?

What forms of self-care do you currently engage in?

What would self-care for your Sun sign look like?

What would self-care for your Moon sign look like?

_____

_____

_____

_____

_____

_____

_____

_____

_____

What would self-care for your Rising sign look like?

_____

_____

_____

_____

_____

_____

_____

_____

_____

Your Moon sign shows you how you need to be cared for.

Astrology Basics: Signs, Houses, and Planets

A birth chart is made up of a three-layered system that includes the signs, the houses, and the planets. In a play or a movie of your life, the planets would be the actors, the signs are the characters that they're playing, and the houses are the sets where the scenes take place.

THE SIGNS

Every sign has things that they're notorious for—these tend to be the imbalanced or shadow aspects of the signs. But there are also the more balanced, higher expressions of every sign that can be considered its strengths or superpowers.

ARIES March 21–April 19
Element: Fire   Quality: Cardinal   Ruling planet: Mars
Superpowers: Independent, initiator, leader, inspiring, direct, decisive, trailblazer
Shadows: Hot-headed, reckless, selfish

TAURUS April 20–May 20
Element: Earth   Quality: Fixed   Ruling planet: Venus
Superpowers: Self-worth, grounded, sensual, dependable, promotes sustainability, stable, generous
Shadows: Stubborn, overindulgent, self-doubt

GEMINI May 21–June 20
Element: Air   Quality: Mutable   Ruling planet: Mercury
Superpowers: Intelligent, expressive, connector, storyteller, multifaceted, witty, versatile
Shadows: Duplicitous, gossip, unreliable

CANCER June 21–July 22
Element: Water   Quality: Cardinal   Ruling planet: Moon
Superpowers: Intuitive, empathetic, receptive, nurturing, supportive, loyal, loving, gentle
Shadows: Moody, suspicious, closed off, defensive, mother issues, insecure

LEO July 23–August 22
Element: Fire   Quality: Fixed   Ruling planet: Sun
Superpowers: Warm, creative, playful, passionate, self-expressive, courageous, giving
Shadows: Self-centered, attention-seeking, dramatic

VIRGO August 23–September 22

Element: Earth   Quality: Mutable   Ruling planet: Mercury

Superpowers: Organized, hardworking, healer, pays attention to detail, discerning, good habits

Shadows: Perfectionist, judgmental, uptight

LIBRA September 23–October 22

Element: Air   Quality: Cardinal   Ruling planet: Venus

Superpowers: Beautifying, balanced, harmonious, objective, diplomatic, considerate, romantic

Shadows: Codependent, dishonest, indecisive

SCORPIO October 23–November 21

Element: Water   Quality: Fixed   Ruling planets: Mars and Pluto

Superpowers: Connects deeply, magnetic, brave, powerful, transformative, passionate, intense

Shadows: Obsessive, controlling, secretive

SAGITTARIUS November 22–December 21

Element: Fire   Quality: Mutable   Ruling planet: Jupiter

Superpowers: Joyful, explorer, has big ideas, searches for meaning, philosopher, honest, optimistic

Shadows: Restless, overzealous, blunt

CAPRICORN December 22–January 19

Element: Earth   Quality: Cardinal   Ruling planet: Saturn

Superpowers: Acts with integrity, structured, determined, achiever, impactful, long lasting, legacy

Shadows: Rigid, workaholic, harsh, father issues

AQUARIUS January 20–February 18

Element: Air   Quality: Fixed   Ruling planets: Uranus and Saturn

Superpowers: Innovative, visionary, hopeful, progressive, revolutionary, individual, equity

Shadows: Aloof, extreme, self-righteous

PISCES February 18–March 20

Element: Water   Quality: Mutable   Ruling planets: Neptune and Jupiter

Superpowers: Deep wisdom, spiritual, psychic, imaginative, adaptable, uplifting, compassionate

Shadows: Escapist, martyr, can dissolve into relationships, isolationist

THE HOUSES

The houses represent areas of life. The planets and the signs that are contained within the houses are the aspects of ourselves that we embody in these areas of our lives.

First—Self, identity, style
Second—Worth, security, possessions
Third—Communication, education, siblings
Fourth—Home, family, roots, inner self
Fifth—Creative expression, pleasure, children
Sixth—Rituals, health, routines, work
Seventh—Partnership, marriage, shadow self
Eighth—Healing, renewal, sex, death, inheritance
Ninth—Philosophy, adventure, teachers
Tenth—Responsibility, recognition, career
Eleventh—Community, groups of friends, hopes, goals
Twelfth—Spirituality, dreams, subconscious, psychic abilities, escapism

THE PLANETS

The planets represent parts of our personality. They can look different depending on the sign and house they show up in on your chart.

Moon—Intuition, emotions, internal world, needs
Sun—Expression, being seen, truth, the self
Mercury—Communication, thoughts, intellect
Venus—Self-worth, love, abundance, values, attraction
Mars—Motivation, action, assertion, sexuality
Jupiter—Surprises, expansion, abundance, search for meaning
Saturn—Lessons, structure, accountability, ambition
Uranus—Revolution, change, inspiration, uniqueness
Neptune—Dreams, spirituality, healing, unconditional love
Pluto—Transformation, life and death cycle, surrender

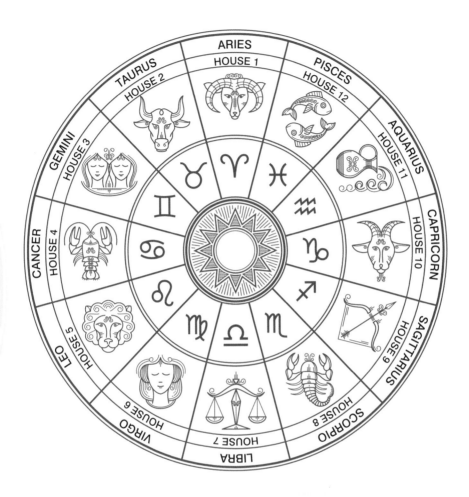

Astrology is a map of your potential in this life.

Think of your Sun sign as the role you're playing in your life, your Rising sign as the genre of your life, and your Moon sign as your internal conflicts—what would the movie of your life look like? (Framework credit: Aliza Kelly)

How could your Rising sign help you embody and express the superpowers of your Sun sign more fully?

Picture your Moon sign showing up to help or care for your Sun and Rising signs. What does that look like? How does it balance them out?

Polarity in astrology is about exploring signs opposite one another to create a balance that's right for you.

How do you connect to your passions and excitement?

How do you get grounded?

How does your environment affect your mood?

Look to the elements of your Sun, Moon, and Rising signs (see page 40) and list them here. Is there any link to the environments you prefer?

Mercury is the planet of expression and communication.

What are your preferred forms of expression and creativity?

How can you share these with your community more?

Saturn is the taskmaster of the zodiac and shows you where you need to put in the work.

What gives you a sense of purpose and satisfaction that's not necessarily your job?

How can you communicate your needs to others in a way that feels both strong and easeful?

Venus and the Moon show us what we need to feel fulfilled, connected, and secure.

What do you feel like you're not getting enough of right now?

_____

_____

_____

_____

_____

_____

_____

_____

_____

_____

How can you generate more of it? How can you make room
for it in your life?

_____

_____

_____

_____

_____

_____

_____

_____

_____

_____

_____

The Ninth House points to our relationship with freedom and the Sixth House reveals how our daily routines and habits show up.

When do you feel the most free?

What does a healthy balance of structure and freedom look and feel like to you?

CHAPTER 6

Herbs & Plant Medicine for Wellbeing

Plants are magic. The leaves, roots, flowers, and fungi found in nature can provide a multitude of benefits to the human body. Creating intentional meals, drinks, or home remedies that contain physical and metaphysical medicine can open us up to a whole new experience in the kitchen and throughout the home.

You are what you eat.

What kinds of herbs are you typically drawn to in meals, teas, or drinks?
(Think basil pesto, chamomile tea, fresh mint in a salad, etc.)

_____

_____

_____

_____

_____

_____

_____

_____

_____

Look up the herbs you're drawn to on pages 116–117. Are there any interesting properties of these herbs that stand out as significant to you? List them here.

_____

_____

_____

_____

_____

_____

_____

_____

_____

_____

What are your family's home remedies for colds, cuts and scrapes, skin care, or low energy? If you don't know of any, look up natural home remedies that you'd like to try. List them all here.

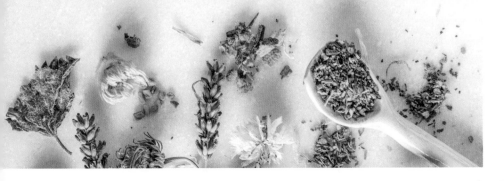

Plants and herbs have the potential to change us on a cellular level.

A KITCHEN WITCH is someone who puts intention and energy into the food and drinks they make for a healing outcome.

Would you like to be a kitchen witch? Why or why not?
What does that look like to you?

A GREEN WITCH is someone who is aligned with the power of the natural world and uses plant remedies to conduct magic and heal.

Would you like to be a green witch? Why or why not?
What does that look like to you?

What types of plants do you have in your home or garden and why do you like these plants?

Essential oils are a great way to embrace plants and herbs without ingesting them. Think of plant scents you find most appealing—optimistic citrus, warming vanilla and cinnamon, grounding wood or trees, calming and encouraging florals.

What smells do you like the most and how could you use a handful of your favorite scents to create a better environment for yourself?

Guide to Magical Plants

The following is a sampling of common herbs and a few you might not have heard of, but most should be easy to find at grocery stores, herbalism shops, or online. Please use organic and responsibly sourced herbs as often as possible. Included are both conventional uses and magical applications, which are often complementary. This list contains just a few uses for each herb. I invite you to do further research before ingesting an herb to make sure it's right for you at this time.

BASIL/SWEET BASIL
Uses: Inflammation, blood cleansing, nausea, anxiety, depression
Magical applications: Abundance, wealth, love, empathy

CHAMOMILE
Uses: Insomnia, digestion, irritability, restlessness, colds
Magical applications: Peace, meditation, purification

DAMIANA
Uses: Tension, anxiety, boosts mood and relaxation
Magical applications: Aphrodisiac, love, visions

HIBISCUS FLOWER
Uses: Healthy blood pressure, boosts heart health and circulation, reduces fluid retention
Magical applications: Openness, pleasure, sensuality, beauty, divination

LEMON BALM
Uses: Stress, nervousness, anxiety, sleep, mood boosting, relaxing
Magical applications: Healing, love, friendship, success, soul soothing

MUGWORT
Uses: Liver tonic, healthy circulation, stomach issues, irregular periods
Magical applications: Strength, spirituality, dreams, healing, psychic powers

NETTLE
Uses: Fatigue, allergies, eczema, stronger hair and bones, aids lactation, boosts metabolism
Magical applications: Protection, nourishment, healing

PARSLEY
Uses: Digestion, heart health, kidney stones, irregular periods, antioxidants
Magical applications: Protection, fertility, shadow work

PEPPERMINT
Uses: Nervousness, headaches, relieves itching and inflammation, memory and alertness
Magical applications: Focus, healing, purification, psychic powers, travel, presence

ROSE
Uses: Pain, depression, heart health, inflammation, bladder infections
Magical applications: Heart opening, healing, luck, love, emotions, prophetic dreams

ROSEMARY
Uses: Boosts cognition, skin protection, digestive and liver health, anxiety, improves mood
Magical applications: Healing, sleep, care, mental ability, youth, purification

SAGE
Uses: Memory and attention, infections, sore throat, hot flashes, sore muscles
Magical applications: Longevity, wisdom, immortality, wishes

SKULLCAP
Uses: Anxiety, insomnia, inflammation
Magical applications: Peace, love, fidelity, stops circular thinking

Of the plants on pages 116–117, which ones are you most excited
to try and why?

How could you use these herbs in your daily rituals?

You can cook with both fresh and dried herbs. They can be sauteed, sprinkled over the top of a finished meal, pureed into a sauce, and more.

Which herbs could you cook with more often and what intentions can they help bring to your meals?

_____

_____

_____

_____

_____

_____

You can also make teas and infusions (which are similar to tea but steeped longer—for about 1–8 hours) with dried or fresh herbs.

Which herbs would you like to create a tea/infusion with and what intentions can they help support?

_____

_____

_____

_____

_____

_____

_____

You can also make infusions to pour into your bath water, and soak up the herbal properties that way.

Imagine your perfect bath. How do you want to feel when you emerge? Which herbs would help support that?

_____

_____

_____

_____

_____

_____

_____

_____

Create a list of all the things that would make your herbal bath even more luxurious. (For example, candles, Epsom salt, music, etc.)

_____

_____

_____

_____

_____

_____

_____

_____

_____

_____

Tuning into your body and figuring out what it needs is a great practice to cultivate. This will open the line of communication between your mind and intuition and help you care for yourself in the best ways possible.

Start by asking your body: How are you today? Write the response you get here.

_____

_____

_____

_____

_____

Follow with: Body, what do you need today?

_____

_____

_____

_____

_____

Your
body
holds
wisdom.

Body, what are you craving in this moment?

Is your body craving a specific food? A type of physical activity or rest? Go a step further and consider if this craving is linked to something deeper. (For example, you might be craving pizza just because it's delicious, but you could also be craving it because it's linked to your sense of connection, togetherness, and comfort.)

List some ways you can give your body the food it's craving, while also satisfying the deeper craving. (Continuing with the pizza example, you could invite a friend or two around to share pizza or play music that reminds you of a sweet memory while you're eating.)

How can you create a daily ritual around checking in with and honoring your cravings?

Plants and herbs can provide support and reinforcement for the healing you're doing with other self-care tools. Think about other work you're doing with this journal, whether it's self-acceptance with astrology in chapter 5, or leaning into the energy of the seasons like in chapter 2.

What do you need on an emotional, physical, and energetic level when delving into these themes?

_____

_____

_____

_____

_____

_____

_____

_____

_____

What plants and their properties would support you in meeting those needs?

_____

_____

_____

_____

_____

_____

_____

_____

_____

_____

_____

Every day for a week, try asking your body: What plant or herb is calling you? Write down the responses you hear/feel and any connections you notice to your health, mood, or external circumstances, as well as something you could do with that plant.

Monday

Tuesday

Wednesday

Thursday

Friday

Saturday

Sunday

WEEKLY REFLECTION:

CHAPTER 7

Healing with Energy Flow & Movement

Energy is the life force that courses through our bodies. It's known throughout cultures by many different things: qi, prana, the breath of life. The term energy work encompasses the practices that help shift us physically, mentally, emotionally, and spiritually. Moving energy through our bodies using tools like breathwork, Reiki, tapping, and intuitive exercise helps your energy to flow, creating multidimensional shifts in your being.

Energy work and movement alchemize our life force by creating internal motion and flow where there were blocks.

How do you already use movement to change how you feel?

_____

_____

_____

_____

_____

_____

_____

_____

_____

Think of a time when you were stressed, burned out, or down and you decided to change how you were feeling by walking around the block or focusing on your breath. What shifts did you notice in your body? Your mental state?

_____

_____

_____

_____

_____

_____

_____

_____

_____

The sympathetic nervous system function is also known as the "fight or flight" response. Part of energy work is about switching from the sympathetic to the parasympathetic nervous system (the "rest and digest") response. An easy way to do this is by controlling your breathing patterns.

When do you experience long periods of stress or anxiety? What takes a toll on you?

When you're stressed, what does your breathing feel like? What's it like when you're relaxed?

Intuitive movement is the practice of tapping into your individual needs on any given day and deciding to move in ways that feel the best to you. This isn't about burning calories, getting six pack abs, or punishing yourself for inactivity or what you ate. This is about honoring your body and doing things that make it feel good.

What types of movement are joyful to you?

Tune into your intuition and ask what forms of exercise are best for you. Write your answers here.

A great way to change your energy with movement is to bring intention to exercise.

List some healthy intentions you can set for exercise. Try writing them as "I" statements in the present tense—for example, "I am strong and secure." Try to use them as mantras when you move (saying them either silently to yourself or out loud).

_____

_____

_____

_____

_____

_____

_____

_____

_____

_____

Movement is a form of alchemy for our internal world.

Where does energy feel stuck for you right now and how long has it felt stuck? How does that stuckness feel to you?

What might be at the root of this blocked energy?

Think of an emotion you often avoid or find ways to ignore when it pops up. What is that emotion and how does it feel when it washes over you?

How could you support yourself in feeling that emotion for 1–2 minutes instead of trying to avoid it?

Personal Energy Work Practice

BREATHWORK

Breathwork, also known as pranayama, is about directing and controlling the breath to support meditative and body practices. It's one of the best and most versatile foundational energy healing practices you can do. It can be done as part of a meditation or movement practice, or on its own, and can help when you're feeling anxious, triggered, or in need of an energy boost. It can move stagnant emotions and be incredibly healing if harnessed in a particular way.

A few breathing techniques:

Simple: Set a timer for 2 minutes. Inhale for 5 counts, and exhale for 5 counts. Repeat as needed. Good for clearing mental chatter, slowing down, calming, and resetting.

The 4-7-8 breath: Start by breathing in for 4 counts, hold for 7, and exhale for 8. This slows down your heart rate, which calms the body while giving the mind something to focus on. Good for sleep and anxiety.

The loud exhale: Breathe into your belly for 4 counts and while exhaling, make any noises you want for as long as you want. It could be a heavy sigh, grunt, laugh, or "ughhh." Good for release, frustration, and anger.

The long game: This is a more dynamic and intense practice, which is done all through the mouth. Breathe into your belly, then inhale again into your chest, then exhale. Repeat at a rhythm for 6–30 minutes. This technique is best done lying down with a recording or practitioner to guide you with music and prompts. Good for releasing stuck emotions and pain and tapping into your inner voice.

Pro tip: You can breathe through the nose or the mouth, unless otherwise stated. You can do breathwork lying down, sitting up, or standing. If lying down, put a pillow under your knees to relieve any stress on the lower back.

REIKI

Reiki is the practice of channeling healing energy through touch or by hovering the hands over the body. Reiki masters perform attunements on students looking to be initiated into Reiki healing, and while it's important to learn the correct ways to use Reiki on others before offering services as a healer, you actually have access to Reiki energy right now. Reiki energy is healing and loving energy from the earth that has the power to shift energy within the physical and emotional body.

Try doing Reiki on yourself. After a meditation, breathwork, or before sleep when your mind is calm, place your hands on your heart, hips, back—wherever you feel needs the most attention. Picture a clear white light coming through the crown of your head, down to your heart, and out through your hands for a few minutes.

Pro tip: Focus on whatever area of the physical or emotional body calls to you. You might not feel the shift immediately, but commit to a week of daily self-Reiki and see how you feel.

TAPPING

Tapping or Emotional Freedom Technique (EFT) works with acupressure points of the body (the tapping sequence can be found easily on YouTube—search Gala Darling's video for a good example). It combines tapping with the fingers on a specific set of points while saying statements out loud in the present tense to assist in releasing blocked emotions and moving energy in the body.

What you say will be a combination of what you want to unblock or release, how it makes you feel, and why you're having issues with it, while consistently coming back to the statement: "But I deeply love, forgive, and accept myself."

You can tap for anything—anxiety, frustration, money issues, conflict, low energy, motivation, accessing joy, etc. Sometimes you'll cry, yawn, cough, or feel your stomach rumble—these are all normal (and temporary) but they are an outward manifestation of moving energy.

Pro tip: Drink plenty of water before and after.

Breathwork is simply breathing with intention. The best part about it is you can take it with you wherever you go and as such, it's a powerful tool for self-healing.

What would it look like to be your own healer?

The next time you're feeling in need of some care or grounding, consider what you can do in the moment for yourself. List a few ideas here—both for breathing and simple self-care. Think of this as your grounding toolkit.

Which of the breathwork patterns on page 134 appeal to you
the most and why?

_____

_____

_____

_____

_____

_____

_____

_____

How could you generate positive change in your inner world by
using your breath?

_____

_____

_____

_____

_____

_____

_____

_____

You have everything you need within you.

**Reiki emphasizes the power of human touch and intention
to create change within.**

Think of a time when you received a hug or a form of loving touch at a time
when you needed it. What effect did it have on you?

_____

_____

_____

_____

_____

_____

_____

_____

You can pour Reiki into your meals, your interactions, and your work.
What would it look like to infuse your day with little Reiki moments?

_____

_____

_____

_____

_____

_____

_____

_____

_____

_____

Try doing self-Reiki daily for a week. Place your hands on wherever you feel like needs attention (see page 135 for full practice) for a few minutes. Do it before you go to sleep or right when you wake up. Record your experience or how you felt afterward here:

Monday

Tuesday

Wednesday

Thursday

Friday

Saturday

Sunday

WEEKLY REFLECTION:

Tapping is called such because you're literally tapping on acupressure points on your body, but you're also tapping into a particular issue within yourself in order to shift it. It can be done daily for anything causing you tension.

List some ways you could benefit from tapping using the following prompts:

What would you like to release?

What would you like to generate more of in your life?

Write out a script for tapping. You don't need to follow this closely when you're tapping, but it's good to have a general idea going into the exercise. Write statements that tap into the emotion and feelings around whatever you're dealing with first, ending each round of tapping with the phrase: "But I deeply love, forgive, and accept myself." Then shift your statements, still in the present, to ways you want to feel instead.

Example: Even though I don't feel confident in myself right now, I'm not sure which direction to go, and I can't seem to find clarity, I deeply love, forgive, and accept myself. I am moving forward with my heart leading the way, I am showing up every day as the most authentic version of me, and I am opening up to new possibilities and solutions.

A lot of self-care comes down to self-acceptance and ultimately, forgiveness. This isn't always easy or simple, and it doesn't mean excusing behavior, but rather setting yourself free from the pain of the past.

Who or what are you ready to forgive?

What older version of yourself are you ready to forgive?

How can you send love to that version of yourself using breathwork, Reiki, tapping, and/or movement?

What are you working toward in your life?

What chapter are you ready to begin?

Transformation
is my constant.